Fascinating INSECTS

Earthworms

Samantha Nugent

LET'S READ
AV²
BY WEIGL™
ADDED VALUE • AUDIO VISUAL

Go to **www.av2books.com**, and enter this book's unique code.

BOOK CODE

S225763

AV² by Weigl brings you media enhanced books that support active learning.

AV² provides enriched content that supplements and complements this book. Weigl's AV² books strive to create inspired learning and engage young minds in a total learning experience.

Your AV² Media Enhanced books come alive with...

Audio
Listen to sections of the book read aloud.

Video
Watch informative video clips.

Embedded Weblinks
Gain additional information for research.

Try This!
Complete activities and hands-on experiments.

Key Words
Study vocabulary, and complete a matching word activity.

Quizzes
Test your knowledge.

Slide Show
View images and captions, and prepare a presentation.

... and much, much more!

Published by AV² by Weigl
350 5th Avenue, 59th Floor New York, NY 10118
Website: www.av2books.com

Library of Congress Control Number: 2015954215

ISBN 978-1-4896-4241-7 (hardcover)
ISBN 978-1-4896-4242-4 (softcover)
ISBN 978-1-4896-4244-8 (multi-user eBook)

Printed in the United States of America in Brainerd, Minnesota
1 2 3 4 5 6 7 8 9 0   19 18 17 16 15

122015
151015

Editor: Katie Gillespie   Art Director: Terry Paulhus

Every reasonable effort has been made to trace ownership and to obtain permission to reprint copyright material. The publishers would be pleased to have any errors or omissions brought to their attention so that they may be corrected in subsequent printings.

Weigl acknowledges Getty Images, Alamy, Corbis, and Minden as the primary image suppliers for this title.

Earthworms

CONTENTS

Meet the earthworm.

Earthworms are small animals.
They have long bodies and no legs.

6

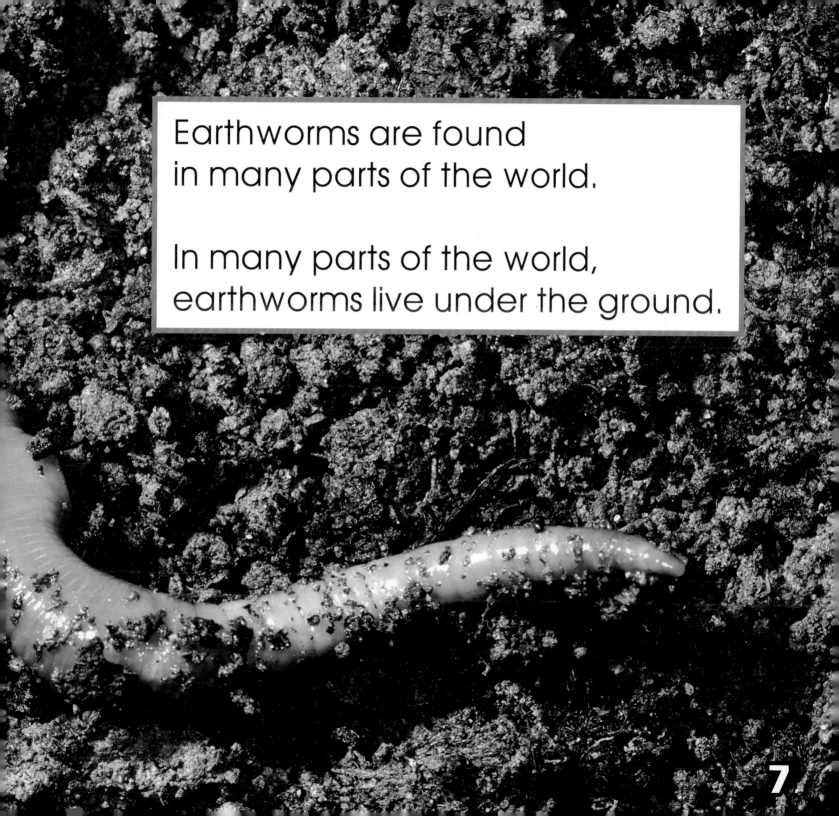

Earthworms are found
in many parts of the world.

In many parts of the world,
earthworms live under the ground.

Earthworms live in wet soil.

In wet soil, earthworms can breathe.

Earthworms are born when they hatch from cocoons.

When they hatch from cocoons, earthworms are thin and white.

Baby earthworms grow when they eat.

When they eat, earthworms can grow longer than a person.

Earthworms squeeze and stretch their bodies.

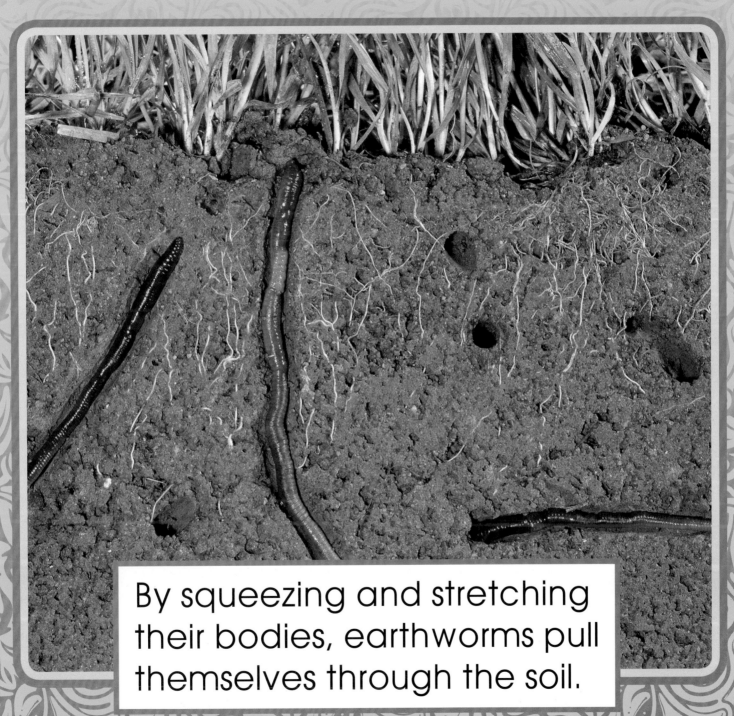

By squeezing and stretching their bodies, earthworms pull themselves through the soil.

16

Earthworms do not have eyes.

With no eyes, earthworms must use their skin to find light.

Earthworms eat soil.

When earthworms eat soil, they make tunnels under the ground.

Earthworms are important in nature.

In nature, earthworms help plants grow.

20

EARTHWORM FACTS

These pages provide more detail about the interesting facts found in the book. They are intended to be used by adults as a learning support to help young readers round out their knowledge of each creature featured in the *Fascinating Insects* series.

Pages 4–5

Earthworms are small animals. They belong to a group of animals called invertebrates. Invertebrates do not have backbones. Insects are also invertebrates, but they differ from earthworms in many ways. One of the most important differences is the earthworm's lack of legs. Insects are commonly identified by the presence of six legs.

Pages 6–7

Earthworms are found in many parts of the world. They live on most continents, including North America, Europe, and Asia. Although earthworms may come to the surface at night, they spend the majority of their lives underground. Depending on their species, earthworms may be found just below the surface or more than 6.5 feet (2 meters) deep in the earth.

Pages 8–9

Earthworms live in wet soil. Unlike animals that use lungs to breathe oxygen from the air, earthworms take in oxygen through their skin. In order to do this, earthworms must stay moist. They are often seen above ground after it has rained. Earthworms can survive in water for weeks at a time, as long as there is enough oxygen for them to breathe. Some species even spend the majority of their lives underwater.

Pages 10–11

Earthworms are born when they hatch from cocoons. When they are ready to lay their eggs, earthworms create small sacs, called cocoons. These cocoons protect the eggs until the babies have finished developing. One to five thin, white babies will hatch from each cocoon. They develop color and begin eating shortly after hatching. If the environment around a cocoon is too dry, the babies may wait more than a year to hatch.

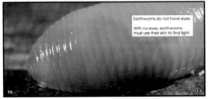

KEY WORDS

Research has shown that as much as 65 percent of all written material published in English is made up of 300 words. These 300 words cannot be taught using pictures or learned by sounding them out. They must be recognized by sight. This book contains 41 common sight words to help young readers improve their reading fluency and comprehension. This book also teaches young readers several important content words. These words are paired with pictures to aid in learning and improve understanding.

Page	Sight Words First Appearance	Page	Content Words First Appearance
4	the	4	earthworm
5	and, animals, are, have, long, no, small, they	5	bodies, legs
7	found, in, live, many, of, parts, under, world	7	ground
9	can	8	soil
10	from, when	10	cocoons
11	white	13	person
12	eat, grow	17	skin
13	a, than	19	tunnels
14	their	20	nature
15	by, through		
17	do, eyes, find, light, must, not, to, use, with		
19	make		
20	help, important, plants